A

DON'T SWEAT
THE SMALL STUFF

Treasury

A
DON'T SWEAT
THE SMALL STUFF
Treasury

A Special Selection
for Fathers

Richard Carlson, Ph.D.

A Don't Sweat the Small Stuff Treasury:
A Special Selection for Fathers

Copyright © 1999, Richard Carlson, Ph.D.

ISBN: 0-7868-6574-1

Library of Congress Catalog Card Number:
99-60271

FIRST EDITION

10   9   8   7   6 · 5   4   3   2   1

Contents

———

Introduction

Without question, two of the happiest days of
my life were the days my two children were born.
Indeed, being a dad is the most important part of
my life, and raising them is, by far, the most significant job I'll ever face. In addition to the obvious
joys of parenting, I also know how difficult and
demanding being a parent can be. I have enormous
respect and gratitude for those dads who take their
job and responsibility as a parent, as well as the gift
of parenting, seriously.

Being a father is an interesting experience. On
the one hand, it brings out the best in you. Most
dads will tell you, "I never knew I could have so
much love for anyone as I do my kids." The old

cliché "I'd do anything for my kids" is almost always true. On the other hand, however, being a dad can sometimes bring out the worst in you. Many dads will also tell you, "I never knew I could get so frustrated and uptight until I was a parent." It's certainly true that kids can drive you crazy, at times—the demands, complaints, noise, bickering, sacrifices, messes, issues, expense, and all the rest can, at times, seem almost too much to handle.

Being a dad is filled with so many truly significant challenges that it's absolutely critical that we learn to avoid sweating the small stuff. We need to learn to let go of the little things, quickly, so that we can focus on the bigger issues as well as the many joys that come with being a dad, the things we often take for granted when we are too stressed out or lost in the flurry of our own busyness.

I have carefully selected strategies from each of

my *Don't Sweat the Small Stuff* books that I have found to be most useful in my own life as a dad, as well as those strategies that dads from all over the world have told me were most helpful to them. These ideas are the ones that have helped me to become more relaxed and joyful around my kids. They are designed to help you bring out the best in your kids as well as yourself. They can help you become a better listener and communicator as well as more patient, supportive, and loving.

I hope this little book is useful to you in your efforts to keep things in perspective and that it assists you in the magical journey of parenting. I thank you from the bottom of my heart for being the best dad you know how to be.

Treasure yourself,

Richard Carlson

The Next Time You Find Yourself in an Argument, Rather than Defend Your Position, See if You Can See the Other Point of View First

—⁂—

It's interesting to consider that when you disagree with someone, the person you are disagreeing with is every bit as certain of his or her position as you are of yours. Yet we always take sides—ours! This is our ego's way of refusing to learn anything new. It's also a habit that creates a lot of unnecessary stress.

The first time I consciously tried the strategy of seeing the other point of view first, I found out something truly wonderful: It didn't hurt, and it brought me closer to the person with whom I was disagreeing.

Suppose a friend says to you, "Liberals [or conservatives] are the major cause of our social problems." Rather than automatically defending your own position (whatever it is), see if you can learn something new. Say to your friend, "Tell me why you think that's true." Don't say this with a hidden agenda or in preparation to defend or prove your position, but simply to learn a different point of view. Don't try to correct or make your friend see how he is wrong. Let your friend have the satisfaction of being right. Practice being a good listener.

Contrary to popular belief, this attitude does not make you weak. It doesn't mean you aren't passionate about your beliefs, or that you're admitting that you're wrong. You're simply trying to see another point of view—you're seeking first to

2

understand. It takes enormous energy to constantly prove a rigid position. On the other hand, it takes no energy to allow someone else to be right. In fact, it's outright energizing.

When you understand other positions and points of view, several wonderful things begin to happen. First, you often learn something new. You expand your horizons. Second, when the person you are talking to feels listened to, he or she will appreciate and respect you far more than when you habitually jump in with your own position. Jumping in only makes him or her more determined and defensive. Almost always, if *you* are softer, the other person will be softer too. It might not happen right away, but in time, it will. By seeking first to understand, you are putting your love and respect for the person to whom you are speaking above your need to be right. You are practicing a form of unconditional love. A side benefit is that the person you are speaking to may even listen to your point of view. While there is no guarantee that he will listen to you, one thing is guaranteed: If you don't listen, he or she won't. By being the first person to reach out and listen, you stop the spiral of stubbornness.

2.

Stop Blaming Others

When something doesn't meet our expectations, many of us operate with the assumption, "When in doubt, it must be someone else's fault." You can see this assumption in action almost everywhere you look—something is missing, so someone else must have moved it; the car isn't working right, so the mechanic must have repaired it incorrectly; your expenses exceed your income, so your spouse must be spending too much money; the house is a mess, so you must be the only person doing your part; a project is late, so your colleagues at work must not have done their share—and on and on it goes.

This type of blaming thinking has become

extremely common in our culture. On a personal level, it has led us to believe that we are never completely responsible for our own actions, problems, or happiness. On a societal level, it has led to frivolous lawsuits and ridiculous excuses that get criminals off the hook. When we are in the habit of blaming others, we will blame others for our anger, frustration, depression, stress, and unhappiness.

In terms of personal happiness, you *cannot* be peaceful while at the same time blaming others. Surely there are times when other people and/or circumstances contribute to our problems, but it is we who must rise to the occasion and take responsibility for our own happiness. Circumstances don't make a person, they reveal him or her.

As an experiment, notice what happens when you stop blaming others for anything and everything in your life. This doesn't mean you don't hold people accountable for their actions, but that you hold *yourself* accountable for your own happiness and for your reactions to other people and the circumstances around you. When the house is a mess, rather than assuming you're the only person doing your part, clean it up! When you're over budget, figure out where *you* can spend less money. Most important, when you're unhappy, remind yourself that only you can make yourself happy.

Blaming others takes an enormous amount of mental energy. It's a "drag-me-down" mind-set that creates stress and disease. Blaming makes you feel powerless over your own life because your happiness is contingent on the actions and behavior of others, which you can't control. When you stop blaming others, you will regain your sense of personal power. You will see yourself as a choice maker. You will know that when you are upset, you are playing a key role in the creation of your own feelings. This means that you can also play a key role in creating new, more positive feelings. Life is a great deal more fun and much easier to manage when you stop blaming others. Give it a try and see what happens.

3.

Become a Less Aggressive Driver

Where do you get the most uptight? If you're like most people, driving in traffic is probably high on your list. To look at most major freeways these days, you'd think you were on a racetrack instead of a roadway.

There are three excellent reasons for becoming a less aggressive driver. First, when you are aggressive, you put yourself and everyone around you in extreme danger. Second, driving aggressively is extremely stressful. Your blood pressure goes up, your grip on the wheel tightens, your eyes are strained, and your thoughts are spinning out of control. Finally, you end up saving no time in getting to where you want to go.

Recently I was driving south from Oakland to San Jose. Traffic was heavy, but moving. I noticed an extremely aggressive and angry driver weaving in and out of the lanes, speeding up and slowing down. Clearly, he was in a hurry. For the most part I remained in the same lane for the entire forty-mile journey. I was listening to a new audiotape I had just purchased and day-dreaming along the way. In enjoyed the trip a great deal because driving gives me a chance to be alone. As I was exiting off the freeway, the aggressive driver came up behind me and raced on by. Without realizing it, I had actually arrived in San Jose ahead of him. All of his weaving, rapid acceleration, and putting families at risk had earned him nothing except perhaps some high blood pressure and a great deal of wear and tear on his vehicle. On average, he and I had driven at the same speed.

The same principle applies when you see drivers speeding past you so that they can beat you to the next stoplight. It simply doesn't pay to speed. This is especially true if you get a ticket and have to spend eight hours in traffic school. It will take you years of dangerous speeding to make up this time alone.

When you make the conscious decision to become a less aggressive driver, you begin using your time in the car to relax. Try to see your driving not only as a way of getting you somewhere, but as a chance to breathe and to reflect. Rather than tensing your muscles, see if you can relax them instead. I even have a few audiotapes that are specifically geared toward muscular relaxation. Sometimes I pop one in and listen. By the time I reach my destination I feel more relaxed than I did before getting into the car. During the course of your lifetime, you're probably going to spend a great deal of time driving. You can spend those moments being frustrated, or you can used them wisely. If you do the latter, you'll be a more relaxed person.

4

Resist the Urge to Criticize

When we judge or criticize another person, it says nothing about that person; it merely says something about our own need to be critical.

If you attend a gathering and listen to all the criticism that is typically levied against others, and then go home and consider how much good all that criticism actually does to make our world a better place, you'll probably come up with the same answer that I do: Zero! It does no good. But that's not all. Being critical not only solves nothing; it contributes to the anger and distrust in our world. After all, none of us likes to be criticized. Our reaction to criticism is usually to become defensive and/or withdrawn. A person who feels attacked is likely to do one of two things: he will either retreat in fear or shame, or he will attack or lash out in anger. How many times have you criticized someone and had them respond by saying, "Thank you so much for pointing out my flaws. I really appreciate it"?

Criticism, like swearing, is actually nothing more than a bad habit. It's something we get used to doing; we're familiar with how it feels. It keeps us busy and gives us something to talk about.

If, however, you take a moment to observe how you actually feel immediately after you criticize someone, you'll notice that you will feel a little deflated and ashamed, almost like *you're* the one who has been attacked. The reason this is true is that when we criticize, it's a statement to the world and to ourselves, "I have a need to be critical." This isn't something we are usually proud to admit.

The solution is to catch yourself in the act of being critical. Notice how often you do it and how bad it makes you feel. What I like to do is turn it into a game. I still catch myself being critical, but as my need to criticize arises, I try to remember to say to myself, "There I go again." Hopefully, more often than not, I can turn my criticism into tolerance and respect.

5

When in Doubt about Whose Turn It Is to Take Out the Trash, Go Ahead and Take It Out

⟶ ∼∽∿∼ ⟵

If we're not careful, it's easy to become resentful about all the responsibilities of daily living. Once, in a very low mood, I figured out that on an average day, I do over 1,000 different things. Of course, when I'm in a better mood, that number is significantly lower.

As I think about it, it's astounding to me how easy it is for me to remember all the chores that I do, as well as all the other responsibilities that I take care of. But, at the same time, it's easy for me to forget all the things that my wife does on a daily basis. How convenient!

It's really difficult to become a contented person if you're keeping score of all you do. Keeping track only discourages you by cluttering your mind with who's doing what, who's doing more, and so forth. If you want to know the truth about it, this is the epitome of "small stuff." It will bring you far more joy to your life to know that you have done your part and someone else in your family has one less thing to do, than it will to worry and fret over whose turn it is to take out the trash.

The strongest argument against this strategy is the concern that you'll be taken advantage of. This mistake is similar to believing it's important that you're right. Most of the time it's *not* important that you're right, and neither is it important if you take the trash out a few more times than your spouse or housemate. Making things like

garbage less relevant in your life will undoubtedly free up more time and energy for truly important things.

6.

Become a Better Listener

~~~

I grew up believing I was a good listener. And although I have become a better listener than I was ten years ago, I have to admit I'm still only an *adequate* listener.

Effective listening is more than simply avoiding the bad habit of interrupting others while they are speaking or finishing their sentences. It's being content to listen to the *entire* thought of someone rather than waiting impatiently for your chance to respond.

In some ways, the way we fail to listen is symbolic of the way we live. We often treat communication as if it were a race. It's almost like our goal is to have no time gaps between the conclusion of the sentence of the person we are speaking with and the beginning of our own. My wife and I were recently at a café having lunch, eavesdropping on the conversations around us. It seemed that no one was really listening to one another; instead they were taking turns not listening to one another. I asked my wife if I still did the same thing. With a smile on her face she said, "Only sometimes."

Slowing down your responses and becoming a better listener aids you in becoming a more peaceful person. It takes pressure from you. If you think about it, you'll notice that it takes an enormous amount of energy and is very stressful to be sitting at the edge of your seat trying to guess what the person in front of you (or on the telephone) is going to say so that you can fire back your response. But as you wait for the people you are communicating with to finish, as you simply listen more intently to what is being said, you'll notice that the pressure you feel is off. You'll immediately feel more relaxed, and so will the people you are talking to. They will feel safe in slowing down their own responses because they won't feel in competition with you for "airtime"! Not only will becoming a better listener make you a more patient person, it will also enhance the quality of your relationships. Everyone loves to talk to someone who truly listens to what they are saying.

7

Imagine Yourself at Your Own Funeral

This strategy is a little scary for some people but universally effective at reminding us of what's most important in our lives.

When we look back on our lives, how many of us are going to be pleased at how uptight we were? Almost universally, when people look back on their lives while on their deathbed, they wish that their priorities had been quite different. With few exceptions, people wish they hadn't "sweated the small stuff" so much. Instead, they wish they had spent more time with the people and activities that they truly loved and less time worrying about aspects of life that, upon deeper examination, really don't matter all that much. Imagining yourself at your own funeral allows you to look back at your life while you still have the chance to make some important changes.

While it can be a little scary or painful, it's a good idea to consider your own death and, in the process, your life. Doing so will remind you of the kind of person you want to be and the priorities that are most important to you. If you're at all like me, you'll probably get a wake-up call that can be an excellent source of change.

8.

Become More Patient

———⟡———

The quality of patience goes a long way toward your goal of creating a more peaceful and loving self. The more patient you are, the more accepting you will be of what is, rather than insisting that life be exactly as you would like it to be. Without patience, life is extremely frustrating. You are easily annoyed, bothered, and irritated. Patience adds a dimension of ease and acceptance to your life. It's essential for inner peace.

Becoming more patient involves opening your heart to the present moment, even if you don't like it. If you are stuck in a traffic jam, late for an appointment, opening to the moment would mean catching yourself building a mental snowball before your thinking got out of hand and gently reminding yourself to relax. It might also be a good time to breathe as well as an opportunity to remind yourself that, in the bigger scheme of things, being late is "small stuff."

Patience also involves seeing the innocence in others. My wife, Kris, and I have two young children ages four and seven. On many occasions while writing this book, our four-year-old daughter has walked into my office and interrupted my work, which can be disruptive to a writer. What I have learned to do (most of time) is to see the innocence in her behavior rather than to focus on the potential implications of her interruption ("I won't get my work done, I'll lose my train of thought, this was my only opportunity to write today," and so forth). I remind myself *why* she is coming to see me—because she loves me, not because she is conspiring to ruin my work. When I remember to see the innocence, I immediately bring forth a feeling of patience, and my attention is brought back to the moment. Any irritation that may have been building is eliminated and I'm reminded, once again, of how fortunate I am to have such beautiful children. I have found that, if you look deeply enough, you can almost always see the innocence in other people as well as in potentially frustrating situations. When you do, you will become a more patient and peaceful person and, in some strange way, you begin to enjoy many of the moments that used to frustrate you.

9

Don't Interrupt Others or Finish Their Sentences

—⟋∿⟍—

It wasn't until a few years ago that I realized how often I interrupted others and/or finished their sentences. Shortly thereafter, I also realized how destructive this habit was, not only to the respect and love I received from others but also for the tremendous amount of energy it takes to try to be in two heads at once! Think about it for a moment. When you hurry someone along, interrupt someone, or finish his or her sentence, you have to keep track not only of your own thoughts but of those of the person you are interrupting as well. This tendency (which, by the way, is extremely common in busy people), encourages both parties to speed up their speech and their thinking. This, in turn, makes both people nervous, irritable, and annoyed. It's downright exhausting. It's also the cause of many arguments, because if there's one thing almost everyone resents, it's someone who doesn't listen to what they are saying. And how can you really listen to what someone is saying when you are speaking for that person?

Once you begin noticing yourself interrupting others, you'll see that this insidious tendency is nothing more than an innocent habit that has become invisible to you. This is good news because it means that all you really have to do is to begin catching yourself when you forget. Remind yourself (before a conversation begins, if possible) to be patient and wait. Tell yourself to allow the other person to finish speaking before you take your turn. You'll notice, right away, how much the interactions with the people in your life will improve as a direct result of this simple act. The people you communicate with will feel much more relaxed around you when they feel heard and listened to. You'll also notice how much more relaxed *you'll* feel when you stop interrupting others. Your heart and pulse rates will slow down, and you'll begin to enjoy your conversations rather than rush through them. This is an easy way to become a more relaxed, loving person.

10

Remind Yourself that When You Die, Your "In Basket" Won't Be Empty

————— ∾∾∾ —————

So many of us live our lives as if the secret purpose is to somehow get everything done. We stay up late, get up early, avoid having fun, and keep our loved ones waiting. Sadly, I've seen many people who put off their loved ones so long that the loved ones lose interest in maintaining the relationship. I used to do this myself. Often, we convince ourselves that our obsession with our "to do" list is only temporary—that once we get through the list, we'll be calm, relaxed, and happy. But in reality, this rarely happens. As items are checked off, new ones simply replace them.

The nature of your "in basket" is that it's *meant* to have items to be completed in it—it's not meant to be empty. There will always be phone calls that need to be made, projects to complete, and work to be done. In fact, it can be argued that a full "in basket" is essential for success. It means your time is in demand!

Regardless of who you are or what you do, however, remember that *nothing* is more important than your own sense of happiness and inner peace and that of your loved ones. If you're obsessed with getting everything done, you'll never have a sense of well-being! In reality, almost everything can wait. Very little in our work lives truly falls into the "emergency" category. If you stay focused on your work, it will all get done in due time.

I find that if I remind myself (frequently) that the purpose of life *isn't* to get it all done but to enjoy each step along the way and live a life filled with love, it's far easier for me to control my obsession with completing my list of things to do. Remember, when you die, there *will* still be unfinished business to take care of. And you know what? Someone else will do it for you! Don't waste any more precious moments of your life regretting the inevitable.

Keep in Mind that a Happy Spouse Is a Helping Spouse

⁓⁓⁓

This is such an obvious concept that I'm almost embarrassed to write about it. Yet, I've found that very few marriages take advantage of the truly remarkable ramifications of this strategy. The idea, of course, is that when your spouse is happy and feels appreciated, he or she will want to be of help to you! On the other hand, when your spouse feels unhappy and/or taken for granted, the last thing in the world he or she will feel like doing is making *your* life easier!

Let me make it perfectly clear that I'm not suggesting that it's your responsibility to make your spouse happy. It's ultimately up to each person to make that happen for himself or herself. We do, however, play a significant role in whether or not our spouses feel appreciated. Think about your own situation for a moment. How often do you *genuinely* thank your spouse for all the hard work he or she does on your behalf? I've met hundreds of people who admit to virtually never thanking their spouses in this way, and almost no one who does so on a regular basis.

Your spouse is your partner. Ideally, you'd treat your partner as you would your best friend. If your best friend, for example, said to you, "I would love to get away by myself for a few days," what would you say? In most cases, you'd probably come back with something like, "That sounds great. You deserve it. You should do it." But if your *spouse* said exactly the same thing, would your reaction be the same? Or would you think about how his or her request would affect you? Would you feel put out, defensive, or resentful? Is a good friend more concerned with himself or herself, or with the happiness of the other person? Do you think it's coincidence that your good friends love to help you whenever possible?

Obviously, you can't always treat your spouse in exactly the same way you would your other good friends. After all, running a marriage and/or a household as well as a joint budget carries with it a great deal of responsibility. However, the dynamic can be similar. For example, if a good friend came over and cleaned your house then took the time to make your dinner, what would you say? How would you react? If your spouse does the very same thing, doesn't he or she deserve the same recognition and gratitude? Most certainly. Whether our jobs involve staying at home, working out of the house, or some combination of the two, we all love and deserve to be appreciated. And when we don't feel taken for granted, our natural instinct is to be of help.

Almost nothing is more predictable than the way people respond when they feel appreciated and valued. Both my wife and I genuinely appreciate each other and try to remember to never take each other for granted. I love it when Kris tells me how much she appreciates all my hard work, and she continues to let me know, even after more than thirteen years of marriage. I also try to remember to acknowledge and express my gratitude daily for her hard work and for her enormous contribution to our family. The result is that we both love to do things for each other—not just out of obligation but because we know that we are appreciated.

You may be doing the same thing already. If so, keep it up. But if not, it's never too late to start. Ask yourself, What could I do to express my gratitude toward my spouse even more than I already do? Usually, the answer is very simple. Make an ongoing effort to say "Thank you," and do so genuinely. Keep in mind not so much what you are doing for the relationship, but what your spouse is doing. Express your gratitude and appreciation. I bet you'll notice what all happy couples do—that the happier and more appreciated your spouse feels, the more often he or she will reach out to help you.

12.

Listen to Her

━━━━◦◦◦━━━━

If I had to pick a single suggestion that was designed to help virtually all relationship and family problems, it would be to become a better listener. And although a vast majority of us need a great deal of work in this area, I'd have to say that it's us *men* who need it the most!

Of the hundreds of women I've known over my lifetime, and the thousands I've spoken to through my work, a vast majority complain that a spouse, boyfriend, significant other, or father is a poor listener. And most say that the slightest improvement in the quality of listening would be extremely well received and would undoubtedly make the relationship, regardless of the nature of the relationship, even better. Listening is almost like a "magic pill" that is virtually guaranteed to produce results.

It's interesting to speak to couples who claim they have a loving relationship. In most cases, if you ask them the secret of their success, they will point to the other person's ability to listen as one of the most significant factors that contributes to the quality of their relationship. This is also true of positive father/daughter, as well as boyfriend/girlfriend, relationships.

Why, then, if the payback is so powerful and certain, do so few of us become good listeners? There are a few reasons that stick out in my mind. First, as far as men are concerned, many of us feel that listening is a nonproactive solution. In other words, when we're listening instead of jumping in, we don't feel as though we're doing anything. We feel we're being too passive. It's hard for us to accept the fact that the listening itself is the solution.

The way to overcome this particular hurdle is to begin to understand how much being listened to is valued by the people we love. When someone genuinely listens to us, it feels as though we are heard and loved. It nourishes our spirits and makes us feel understood. On the other hand, when we don't feel listened to, our hearts sink. We feel as though something is missing; we feel incomplete and dissatisfied.

The other major reason so few of us become good listeners is that we don't realize how bad we really are! But, other than someone telling us about it or pointing it out to us in some way, how would we know? Our poor listening skills become an invisible habit that we don't even realize we have. And because we have so much company, our listening skills probably seem more than adequate—so we don't give it much thought.

Determining how effective you are as a listener takes a great deal of honesty and humility. You have to be willing to quiet down and listen to yourself as you jump in and interrupt someone. Or you have to be a little more patient and observe yourself as you walk away, or begin thinking of something else, before the person you are speaking to has finished.

This is about as close as you're going to get to a virtually guaranteed result. You may be amazed at how quickly old problems and issues correct themselves and how much closer you will feel to the ones you love if you simply quiet down and become a better listener. Becoming a better listener is an art form, yet it's not at all complicated. Mostly, all it requires is your intention to become a better listener, followed by a little practice. I'm sure your effort will be well worth it!

13

Think of Taking Care of Your Home Like Painting the Bridge

—◦◦◦—

An architect once told me something that truly amazed me about the amount of work it took to maintain the Golden Gate Bridge in the San Francisco Bay Area. He said the bridge is painted virtually every day of the year. In other words, by the time the work is done, it's time to start over. It's never done! Instead, it's literally an ongoing process. Furthermore, in the absence of this constant care, the bridge would be in jeopardy of expensive wear and tear as well as more cosmetic consequences.

One day it dawned on me that taking care of a home is much like painting this extraordinary bridge. And thinking of it in these terms has been an enormous relief in my life.

Like most people, I used to get overwhelmed about the care and maintenance of our home. If something was in need of repair or disorganized, it would make me nervous and frustrated. Looking back, it seems that I was frustrated most of the time, because it seemed like something was always wrong with our home—a sink needed repair, a room needed paint, the attic needed cleaning, the dishes needed to be washed, a closet was a mess, weeds needed to be pulled, and so forth. It was as if I felt that there would come a time when it would somehow all be done. And, I fantasized, when it was finally finished, I'd be able to feel relaxed and satisfied.

Well, several years later, the house is still "in process." The weeds still need to be pulled, the attic still gets messy, dishes are still in the sink, and my daughters' rooms need paint once again! In a way, it's exactly like the Golden Gate Bridge. It's never done—and it never will be. The only difference is that now I understand and have accepted this fact about having a home.

Looking at my home in this way has been a tremendous relief. Now, instead of panicking or overreacting when something isn't finished or needs to be done, I'm able to keep it in much better perspective. I'm not suggesting that I don't work hard to keep things in good repair and orderly—I do, only I'm not nearly as attached to completing the project.

My guess is that if you look at your home in this way it will be a tremendous source of relief. In all likelihood, you'll have even greater appreciation for the things that do get finished and less frustration over those things that don't.

14

Develop Your Own Reset Buttons

———⟋⟍⟋⟍———

In every household there are warning signals that have the potential to alert us when chaos is just around the corner. The problem is, we rarely listen to these signals. Instead, we go about our business until the chaos overwhelms us. We can avoid a vast majority of this sense of being overwhelmed, however, by listening to these warning signals and learning to use them as reset buttons.

For example, one of the warning signals in our home occurs when all four of us are feeling rushed. There is an undeniable frenzied feeling that occurs when everyone feels pressured for time and seems to be rushing around, frustrated. As a family, we have learned to recognize this feeling and to treat it as a reset button. In other words, one of us will notice the feeling and say something like, "Hey, gang, here we go again," or something to this effect. This simple recognition allows us to take a breath, slow down, and in effect, start over or reset our speed. Virtually always, this warning signal is trying to tell us that we all need to slow down and regroup.

By using this reset procedure, we can regroup and regain our bearings and perspective, thereby allowing us to start over. On those occasions when we fail to listen to or pay attention to this warning signal, the feeling in our home becomes even more speeded up and usually leads to a great deal of frustration.

Other common warning signals include heated arguments between siblings. You can use the argument itself as an opportunity to reset the mood and atmosphere. Rather than waiting for a full-blown fight, take action before it gets out of control—use the early warning signs as your reset button. If you have only one child, you might consider whining in a similar light. If you live alone, a reset button might occur when there are too many items in your "in basket" or when there are too many dishes piled up in the sink. The potential list is vast, and your reset buttons will be unique. The idea is to see the stress coming before it actually arrives, to nip it in the bud.

Think about your own home for a moment. Are there predominant or recurring patterns of stress? If so, are there warning signals that precede the stress? If you look carefully, you'll probably see that there are. The trick is to use those signals to your advantage. Pay attention to them and use them as reset buttons. If you do, you'll notice far less stress in your home.

15

Never, Ever, Take Your Spouse (or Significant Other) for Granted

—————

I could write an entire book on this subject. But, since I have only a few paragraphs to explain, I'll get right to the heart of the matter.

If you take your spouse for granted, it is absolutely 100 percent guaranteed to adversely affect your relationship. I've never, ever, met a single person who likes to be taken for granted—and very few who will put up with it, over the long run.

Clearly, one of the most disrespectful and destructive things we can possibly do to our spouses (or anyone) is to take them for granted. To do so is sort of like saying, "It's your job to make my life easier and my job to expect it." Ouch!

There are so many ways we take *our* partners for granted. Here are just a few: We take our roles more seriously than theirs. We think our contributions are significant and that our partners are "the lucky ones." Many of us forget to say please and thank-you—some of us never do. We fail to reflect on how lucky we are or how sad and difficult it would be to live without our spouses. Sometimes we get very demanding of our spouses or treat them much differently than we would a friend. Other times, we speak "for them" or disrespectfully about them in front of others. Some of us think we know what our spouses are thinking, so we make decisions for them. Then there is the common mistake of coming to expect certain things—a clean home or a hot meal. Or money to pay the bills, or a nice clean-cut lawn. They are, after all, our spouses. They should do these things. Finally, very few of us really listen to our spouses or share in their excitement—unless, of course, it matches something *we* are interested in. I could go on and on, but you get the point.

Is it any wonder that close to 50 percent of marriages end in divorce and that many of the rest are painful, boring, and/or less than satisfying? Hardly! It's so obvious, but for some reason we keep making the same mistake—we take our partners for granted.

The reverse is also true—almost nothing makes people feel better than feeling as though they are appreciated and valued. Think about how wonderful it felt when you first met your spouse or significant other. It was absolutely wonderful. And a major contributing factor to this feeling of love you shared was that you truly appreciated each other. You said things like "It's so nice to hear from you" and "Thank you for calling." You expressed your appreciation for everything from a simple compliment to the tiniest gift, card, or gesture of kindness. Each chance you had, you expressed your gratitude, and you never took your new love for granted.

Many people believe that it's inevitable that couples will lose their sense of appreciation for one another. Not so! Appreciation is something you have 100 percent control over. If you choose to be grateful and to express your appreciation, you will do so. And the more you do so, the more you'll be in the healthy habit of noticing things to be grateful for—it's a self-fulfilling prophecy.

My wife, Kris, is one of the most appreciative people I've ever known. She's constantly telling me how much she loves me or how lucky she is to be married to me. I try to remember to do the same because that's exactly how I feel. And you know what? Every time she expresses her appreciation toward me, I feel that much more love for her. And she assures me the same is true for her. But we don't do this as a way of getting love, but simply because we both tend to focus on how lucky we are to have one another as a friend and partner.

For example, I'll be away at a speaking engagement and Kris will leave me a sweet message telling me how grateful she is that I'm willing to work so hard for our family. About the same time, I'll leave a message with her, letting her know how grateful I am that she's willing and able to be home with our children, giving them the love they need and deserve, while I'm away. We both honestly feel that the other is making at least an equal sacrifice and that, regardless, we're on the same team. Then, when she's away and I'm home, it seems that we reverse compliments. She's grateful that I'm willing and able to be at home and I'm equally grateful that she's away making yet another contribution to our family.

Kris and I have been together for more than fifteen years, and we love each other more today than we did all those years ago. I'm absolutely certain that our decision to *not* take each other for granted is one of the major reasons why this is true. I'll bet you'll be shocked at how powerful this strategy can be if you give it a try. For the time being, forget what you are getting back and focus only on what you are giving. I believe that if you make the decision to stop taking your partner for granted, in time your spouse will begin to do the same thing. It feels good to be grateful. Try it, you'll love it!

Appreciate Your In-Laws

〰〰〰

Admittedly, this has been an easy one for me because my in-laws, Pat and Ted, are extraordinary people. And I must say that my wife is equally lucky because my parents are also quite special. However, for many people, in-laws present quite a personal challenge, to say the least. And even if you like your in-laws, you do have to make certain sacrifices simply because of the nature of marriage. You will, for example, have to make trade-offs as to where you spend holidays. You will also have to deal with the almost unavoidable problems of conflicting backgrounds and upbringings—different religious philosophies, differing views on parenting, discipline, spending, saving, the relative importance of spending time with family, and so forth. Yet, despite the probable differences among you, I believe that most in-law relationships have the potential to be loving and filled with mutual respect.

The trick to making the most of your relationship with your in-laws is to stay focused on gratitude. While there almost certainly will be differences you will have to deal with, gratitude will enable you to appreciate, rather than struggle against, those differences.

It's easy to forget, yet if you love your spouse, you owe your in-laws an enormous debt of gratitude! If not for their bringing your spouse into the world, you would be with someone else, or alone. In most instances, it took your in-laws (or one of them) to raise your spouse. So, regardless of what you may think, they played a significant role in your spouse's upbringing.

Before you sarcastically think something like "That explains why my spouse has certain problems," keep in mind that the opposite is equally true. If you blame your in-laws for any issues your spouse struggles with, it's only fair to give them credit for his or her strengths as well. In addition, if you have children, their genes—their physical makeup—come, in part, from your in-laws. Without their contribution, your children would not be the people they are. If you think your kids are cute, and who doesn't think so, some of that cuteness, whether you want to believe it or not, comes from your in-laws.

Believe me, I'm not a bury-your-head-in-the-sand-and-pretend-that-everything-is-perfect kind of person. I realize that all in-laws have certain difficult qualities, just as I will to my future son-in-law, someday down the road (way down the road). However, what choice do you have? You can continue to complain about your in-laws, make mean-spirited jokes about how difficult it is to have them, and wish that they were different—or you can begin to focus less on their irritating quirks and characteristics and instead focus on that which you have to be grateful for. I believe the decision is an easy one. Stay focused on gratitude and my guess is that you'll be able to improve your existing relationship in a significant way.

17

Separate Work from Everything Else

———

Like millions of people, and despite having an office outside the home, I also work a great deal at home. In fact, I'm writing this sentence in my upstairs office before the sun has started to rise.

There are few things more predictable than the stress you create for yourself when you fail to separate your work from the rest of your life. I don't mean you shouldn't work at home, only that you should take steps toward separating your work from the rest of your life.

If you're going to work at home, if at all possible have a separate phone line and a room that is dedicated solely to your work. I've heard many people say, "It's not worth the extra expense to have a separate phone line." What these people aren't taking into consideration is the fact that many people are annoyed by businesses whose phones are answered by someone other than the person associated with the business. For example, despite being a pretty easygoing person, I have to admit that I find it a little disconcerting when I'm trying to reach someone (on whom I'm going to spend money) and a child answers the phone, or a spouse who has little or no knowledge of what's going on. I often wonder if the person I'm trying to reach is really going to get my message! Sometimes, it's just easier to find someone else who makes the effort to make my experience (as the customer) an easier one. It's very possible that you could actually lose customers or future referrals by mixing your personal phone line with that

of your business. In most cases, one lost custo|
is going to cost far more than a monthly service
charge from your phone company.

But beyond your phone, there's the "organiza-
tion factor." The more you are able to keep your
work separated from your home life, the less often
you'll lose or misplace things. You'll know where
to find your date book, your projects, phone num-
bers, and other important information. Things
won't be so likely to get mixed up. You'll think of
your work space as just that—your work space.
And your home will be yours to enjoy. You'll feel
more organized and less stressed out.

When you combine your work space with your
living space—when you share a phone, carry
papers around the house, work in different
rooms—you'll be far more inclined to make social
calls and do other, nonwork-related, activities than

you would if you kept everything separate. The reason for this is obvious—you're used to calling your friends in the living room, or tidying up while you're in the kitchen. By keeping everything separate, however, you'll be far more productive and waste less time.

I have learned to keep my work separate from everything else. My kids aren't allowed to play on my laptop computer, nor are they allowed to play with my files or use my fax machine. The result of my conscious effort to keep everything separate is that I'm not only more productive but, in addition, I'm substantially less stressed out than I used to be when I allowed my home and work lives to be one and the same. My guess is that, if you give this strategy a try, you'll be far less inclined to sweat the small stuff at home because you'll be less nervous about the consequences of mixing your work with the rest of your life. Now that I've finished writing this section, I think I'll go downstairs and see what the kids are doing!

18

Don't Overemphasize Your Vacations

———⁙———

Obviously, a vast majority of life is *not* spent on vacation. Yet, many of us emphasize the importance of our vacations so much that we forget to enjoy the rest of our lives, our day-to-day, moment-to-moment experiences. We plan and look forward to our vacations, sometimes as if they were the only part of life worth really living. We build up our expectations that our time off is going to be the highlight of our year, a saving grace that will make up for all the hassle and disappointment of our daily lives. We think to ourselves, "Boy, life is going to be great once we get there."

There are several problems with this overemphasis on vacation. First, as I have already suggested, vacation represents a tiny percentage of our overall lives. Most people I know spend a week or two, at most, on vacation. The rest of the time it's business as usual. To spend fifty weeks a year planning and longing for the other two is a classic example of reversed priorities, an exercise in almost guaranteed frustration. Part of the problem is that, when your primary emphasis is on later, your mind is removed from the present moment. Instead of being fully engaged in the here and now, and discovering joy in daily living, your focus is on how much better things will be and how much more fun you'll be having *later*—instead of now.

Another problem with extremely high expectations is that, in many instances, they are unrealistic, which can lead to a great deal of disappointment. Recently, Kris and I fell into this trap. It had been a particularly busy time and we hadn't had a chance to get away during the summer. We did, however, plan a mini-trip to the beach that we were really looking forward to. In my mind, this trip was going to be so great that it would make up for our lack of travel during the summer. I anticipated laughing children, appreciation for one another, and lots and lots of fun. However, what had been paradise in my mind turned out to be quite a hassle. It had been a while since all of us had been in one small hotel room together. It was crowded, and hot, and the kids argued more than usual. They disagreed about how we were going to spend our time, and Kris and I felt trapped in the middle. The beach was crowded and so was the pool, and the weather, of course, did not cooperate. In short, all of us realized that, at least this time, we really had more fun, space, and enjoyment back at our own home.

Please don't misunderstand me. I'm not suggesting that there's anything wrong with vacations or that looking forward to them is a mistake. I'm also aware that many vacations, including a vast majority of my own, are wonderful. What I'm attempting to alert you to is the common problem of making a bigger deal out of your vacations than is really necessary, of overemphasizing how great somewhere else is going to be instead of remembering how special and terrific your life is right where you are. I can guarantee you that if, instead of relying on your vacations to make you happy, you learn to be more contented and peaceful wherever you are, when you do get on your vacation, it too will be a rich experience—most of the time.

Of course, the reverse is also true. If you're unhappy and stressed out a vast majority of the time, it's unrealistic to believe that, once you get on vacation, you'll be relaxed and calm. My advice is simple: Go ahead and plan your vacation, and when you get there have a great time. But never forget that ordinary life can also become quite extraordinary if you remember to be grateful for what you already have.

19

Remind Yourself that You Can't Take It with You

—~~~—

Unless you know something I don't, when you die you will leave your home and *all* your possessions behind. Despite this rather obvious observation, many of us fail to live as if this were true. Instead, we spend a huge amount of our time and energy tending to—dusting, caring for, purchasing, insuring, protecting, taking care of, showing off—our stuff, as if it had some lasting value.

It's incredibly helpful to remind yourself that you can't take any of it with you! This doesn't suggest that you shouldn't enjoy your things while you're here—you most certainly should. Instead, it's a gentle reminder to keep things in perspective and ask yourself, "What's *really* most important here?" Ask questions like "Is it absolutely necessary that the bathroom get cleaned this very minute, or is it more important [and more nurturing] to take a walk with my spouse [or child or dog]?" Let me reiterate. I'm *not* implying that the bathroom doesn't need to be cleaned, only that it's helpful to keep its relative importance in mind. There will be times when cleaning the bathroom will take precedence over a walk in woods—and that's okay too.

I can almost guarantee you that someday, as you look back on your life, you'll be less interested in how many items and achievements you were able to collect than in how much you were able to express love, spend time with the people you care most about, and contribute to the world you live in. Acknowledging this truth *right now* can help you prioritize your goals and your time in a way that nurtures your spirit. It can be the difference between a superficial life and a life of substance.

Your home is an important part of your life. You live in your home. You spend a great deal of time there. You eat meals, share with family and friends, and rest—all at home. It's critical to remember, however, that the love we share in our home is what's most important—not the home itself, not the stuff. If something gets broken or needs repair, so be it. If the house is a mess or disorganized, do the best you can. Keep your reactions in perspective. Your things and your home are here to enjoy and to make your life easier and more comfortable. But don't give them the authority to overwhelm you. By reminding yourself that you can't take any of it with you, you open a new door of acceptance and freedom.

20

Get Some Exercise

———∽∽∽———

I'd estimate that at least half the people I know get little or no exercise. The excuses range from "I don't have time" to "It's too hard' and "I don't enjoy it."

While I'm certainly no expert on the advantages of exercise, I have enjoyed exercise for as long as I can remember. From my perspective, the only valid excuse for not exercising on a regular basis is the physical inability to do so. Other than that, as far as I'm concerned, if you don't get any exercise you're shooting yourself in the foot! You're missing out on an easy and effective way to become happier, less reactive, and more peaceful, and you're putting yourself at an unfair, yet totally unnecessary, disadvantage when having to deal with the inevitable hassles and challenges of life at home.

In a very real way, I feel I don't have time to *not* exercise—nor do I feel I can afford the luxury of not doing so. It would be very difficult for me to justify not doing something that makes me feel terrific and has the added benefit of keeping me healthy, fit, and calm—as well as providing me with tons of extra energy. Regular exercise has proven benefits of releasing endorphins, which have a calming effect on the brain and in your body. After exercising, many of the small things that drive you crazy would have little or no negative impact on you. And even the truly big things would be a little easier to deal with.

It's true that from a very narrow perspective, and in the very short term, exercise does take some time (I spend forty-five minutes to one hour, five or six days a week). However, that's an awfully small price to pay if you spend less time sick and/or in the hospital, and your day-to-day energy level and ability to be productive are increased substantially. It's also a small price to pay if you consider how much mental energy it take to be annoyed and bothered by day-to-day things around the house. Just think how much better your life would seem if you could become even a little bit less reactive and more efficient as the result of getting a little regular exercise! Then there's your fitness to consider. To put it bluntly, a physically fit body looks and feels a lot better than one that is seldom used! Finally, while I can't prove this is the case, I know that I tend to sleep a whole lot better at night when I'm getting regular exercise.

I know, I know. It's hard to get started, and there are hundreds of great excuses. You should know, however, that in this past year alone I've met two incredible people—one in a wheelchair and another with very severe physical handicaps—both of whom are regular exercisers. Both also work full-time, and both have families to care for.

What have you really got to lose? I suggest and sincerely hope you'll give exercise a try—find something you enjoy: walking, jogging, hiking, biking, even running in place at home or on a treadmill. Do something. My guess is that, immediately, you'll be sweating the small stuff far less at home, and, in time, you'll think it was one of the best decisions you've ever made.

21

Reverse Roles with Your Spouse

—————

It's sad, yet the easiest person to take for granted is probably the person you love most in the world—your spouse. It's so easy to get lost in your own world and set of real-life responsibilities that you begin to believe that your spouse has it much easier than you do, or you forget (or perhaps don't even realize) how hard your spouse works on your behalf. This tendency can create a great deal of resentment yet is, to a large degree, very preventable. The key to prevention is to put yourself in your spouse's shoes.

I'm going to give an example here *knowing* that there are millions of exceptions to this stereotype.

I'm aware that in today's world many, if not most, families have two income earners and that many, if not most, families share many of the responsibilities at home. I'm also aware that women are often the ones who work while men stay home with the kids. See if you can see through my stereotypical examples, however, to the heart of this important message.

Many of my own male friends have fallen into the trap of taking their spouses for granted. I'm happy to report, however, that some have been helped by taking this strategy to heart. A common example is a man who works and is married to a woman who stays at home (and of course she works hard too). In this typical chauvinistic example, the husband convinces himself that his wife is lucky and often minimizes the importance of her role. He believes her needs are being met while he's out working all day. He rarely contributes much at home in the way of chores, children, and household responsibilities. He feels put out when asked to do the simplest of things. He's absolutely aware of how hard he works but takes his wife's role completely for granted.

It's shocking (but often very good for a marriage) in cases like this for the husband to take over the home for a week, or even a few days, while his wife visits friends and takes a break. Many men are so frightened by this suggestion that they get the point before they are actually forced to go through the experience. They often realize, when push comes to shove, that they are absolutely incapable of doing the important daily tasks of running a home and raising children. They also realize how exhausting it can be. This is truly hard work! The idea, of course, in switching roles is to regain a sense of gratitude as well as compassion for what one person does for the other.

Of course, this strategy works both ways. It's also very common for a stay-at-home mom to take her husband for granted. She might, for example, complain about late nights or missed dinners without fully realizing how difficult it can be to earn a living. In most instances, it's unrealistic for a nonworking spouse to actually reverse roles for a week. However, she (or he) could really benefit from trying to imagine what it would be like to actually go out and earn enough money to satisfy the financial needs of her (or his) family. This can be a shocking realization for someone who doesn't actually have a job.

The point of this mental exercise is not to determine whose job is more difficult or important but to recognize the importance and inherent difficulty in both aspects of life. Regardless of your personal sitation, and even if you and your spouse both work and both help out at home, it can be enormously helpful to experiment and play around with this strategy. If you do, I think you'll begin to realize and appreciate how much your spouse does for you and how difficult his or her life can be at times. And I can assure you that everyone loves to be appreciated; when people are appreciated, they are more fun to be around.

22

Make Friends with Your Receptionist

Not too long ago I was in San Francisco in a reception lounge, waiting for my lunch partner. I was lucky enough to be a witness to the following chain of events which were so to the point of this book, I immediately knew I would like to share them with you.

A man walked in and barked out, in an unfriendly and demanding tone, "Any messages?" The female receptionist looked up and smiled. In a pleasant tone she answered, "No, sir." He responded in a nasty, almost threatening manner, "Just be sure to call me when my twelve-thirty appointment arrives. Got it?" He stormed down the hall.

No more than a minute later, a woman entered the room who apparently also wanted to know if she had any messages. She smiled, said "hello," and asked the receptionist if she was having a nice day. The receptionist smiled back and thanked the woman for asking. She then proceeded to hand the woman a stack of messages and shared with her some additional information which I could not hear. They laughed together a few times before the woman thanked the receptionist and walked down the hall.

It's always shocked me when I've seen someone who isn't friendly to the receptionist or who takes him or her for granted. It seems like such an obviously short-sided business decision. Over the years I've asked many receptionists whether or not they treat everyone in the office equally. Most of the time I receive a response such as, "You're kidding, right?" Indeed, it seems that receptionists have a great deal of power—and being friendly to them can make your life a lot easier. Not only does being nice to your receptionist all but ensure a friendly hello and someone to trade smiles with a few times a day, but in addition, your receptionist can do a great many intangible things for you—protect your privacy and screen calls, remind you of important events, alert you to potential problems, help you prioritize and pace yourself, and on and on.

I've seen both ends of the spectrum. I've seen receptionists protect people they work with from a variety of unnecessary hassles, even save them from major mistakes. I once saw a receptionist run down the hall and all the way down the street to remind someone of a meeting she was sure the person was going to forget. I later asked the person who was chased to tell me what had happened. He verified at the receptionist had been his "hero." He went so far as to claim that she may have even saved his job. When I asked this receptionist about their rapport, she informed me that they weren't really friends, but that he was an extremely nice person. I asked her if that had anything to do with her willingness to run down the street in the hot sun to remind him of a meeting. She just smiled and said, "You get right to the point, don't you?"

Sadly, the opposite can occur when a receptionist feels taken for granted or resentful of someone. I've heard stories of receptionists who have mysteriously "lost" messages, or who have failed to remind someone of a meeting, because it was inconvenient to do so.

Obviously, there are plenty of great receptionists who are able to set aside their personal feelings and do what is best, most if not all of the time. But think about this issue from the perspective of the recep tionist. He or she might answer the phone, respond to the messages for a relatively large number of people, and have a number of other important responsibilities. Some of the people they work with are really nice, most are moderately so, and a few are jerks. Isn't it obvious that being friendly to your receptionist is in your best interest? Aside from the fact that it's their job, what possible motivation does a receptionist have to go the extra mile, or do something they aren't officially being paid to do, if you aren't nice to them—or at very least respectful?

In no way am I suggesting that you make friends with your receptionist just to get something in return. Primarily, you want to do so simply because it's a nice thing to do and because it will brighten the workday for both of you. After all, your receptionist is someone you see on a daily basis. But aside om that, it's just good business and it takes so little time or effort. My suggestion is to think of your receptionist as a key partner in your life. Treat them as if you truly value them—as you should. Be kind, genuine, patient, and courteous. Thank them when they do something for you—even if it's part of their job. Can you imagine the stress and other possible consequences of missing just one of those important phone calls—or a single important message? It's your receptionist who prevents that from happening. Wouldn't it seem wise to include your receptionist on your holiday shopping list? Incidentally, the same principle applies to many other roles as well, in different ways—the janitor, housecleaner, managers, cook, and so on.

I think you'll find that making friends with your receptionist is a wise thing to do. It's a great way to brighten your day-to-day work life, as well as an effective way to make your life a little less stressful. If you haven't already done so, I encourage you to give it a try.

23

Recognize Patterns of Behavior

—◦◦◦◦—

No matter where you work or what you do, becoming an expert in recognizing patterns of behavior can help you reduce the stress in your life by eliminating many of your unnecessary interpersonal conflicts. It will also help you to keep your perspective by being less surprised when "stuff happens." When you learn to recognize patterns of behavior, you'll be able to detect problems before they have a chance to get out of hand, nip certain arguments in the bud, and prevent hassles that might otherwise manifest themselves.

If you take a careful look at the people you work with, you'll probably agree that most people (you and I too) have a tendency to repeat patterns and engage in habitual reactions. In other words, we tend to be bothered by the same things, irritated by the same sets of circumstances, argue over the same sets of facts, and act defensively toward certain types of behavior. Indeed, for most of us, our reactions to life, particularly stress, are fairly predictable.

This being the case, it's enormously helpful to take careful note of the people you work with—and recognize any negative or destructive patterns of behavior that are likely to repeat themselves. You might notice, for example, that if you take on or challenge a member of your team, he will become defensive and tend to argue. This doesn't mean it's never appropriate to challenge him—there will certainly be times when it is. What it means is that when you recognize, with relative certainty, what's going to happen if you engage in certain types of interactions, you might determine that it's not worth getting into. In this way, you can avoid unnecessary conflict and spend your time and energy in more efficient ways. In order to be able to do this, of course, you'll have to take an honest look at your own patterns of behavior. Perhaps you're the one who starts some of the arguments, or you are a willing participant once they get going.

Maybe there is someone in your office who is virtually incapable of completing a project on time—he's always a day or two late. He's always got a great and legitimate-sounding excuse, yet the end result is always the same—he's late. By being aware of the pattern and the virtual certainty with which it occurs, you may be able to protect yourself, or at least be less frustrated by it. You can attempt to avoid participating in projects with him where on-time performance is a must. If working with him can't be avoided, you can try to build in some extra time, or get off to an early start, knowing full well what is likely to occur. And in a worst-case scenario, you will probably be less stressed out by his lateness because you already knew it was going to happen.

Perhaps someone else you work with gets argumentative when she feels criticized. If you recognize this particular pattern of behavior, you might think twice before offering habitual advice that she is likely to receive as criticism. Again, if it's necessary and appropriate to criticize or offer advice, that's a completely different story. What I'm referring to here is the daily, habitual types of comments that lead to hard feelings and unnecessary conflict.

Maybe a friend or coworker is someone who loves to gossip. By recognizing this pattern of behavior, you can avoid a great deal of potential grief and stop rumors before they have a chance to start. You begin to realize that if you share a story with her, she *is* going to share that story with others. It doesn't matter whether you ask her not to— or that she promises that she won't—or that her intentions are pure. This doesn't mean she's a bad person, only that her pattern is that she can't help but gossip. If you recognize the pattern, you have an enormous edge. You can bite your tongue and keep your secrets to yourself when you are with her, unless you really don't mind her sharing them with others. And if you make the decision to go ahead and tell her something, don't get upset when others discover your secret. It was predictable. It's part of the pattern.

I could go on and on. A person who is cheap is almost always cheap. Someone who gets jealous usually does so on a consistent basis. Someone else who steals the glory does so whenever the opportunity presents itself. A person who is dishonest tends to be dishonest whenever it seems to suit his needs. Someone who is hypersensitive will likely feel criticized, regardless of how gentle you attempt to be. An individual who is consistently late will probably show up late even though you've asked her not to—and so forth. Once you witness the pattern, whatever it is, it's a bit self-destructive to feed into it.

By recognizing patterns of behavior, you are in the driver's seat at work. This type of reflective wisdom allows you to better choose what to say and what not to say; who to spend time with and who to avoid, when possible. It helps you make he decision "not to go certain places" with certain people. Starting today, take a careful look at the patterns of behavior where you work. You'll be less stressed-out very soon.

24.

Take Your Next Vacation at Home

This is a strategy I began using a number of years ago. To be honest, the first few times I gave it a try, I felt sure I was going to be giving up something—fun, relaxation, "my big chance to get away"—and that I would end up disappointed. However, I can honestly say that every time I stayed home for my vacation, I'm really glad I did. Never once have I regretted my decision.

Vacations are something most people look forward to. They are usually wonderful, well-deserved, and almost always needed. However, a vacation which is ideally designed to be relaxing, rejuvenating, and energizing can at times bring on more stress

...an it eliminates. Here's a scenario. You finally get a week off. You have a great trip planned, yet you still have to do all that's necessary to leave. You rush to pack and to get all the loose ends and assorted details attended to. You're exhausted. It feels like you haven't had a chance to sit still for weeks. Yet here you are, running to catch another airplane, or rushing out the door to avoid traffic. In a way it seems like you're *speeding up so that you can slow down*. You want to get the most out of your vacation, so you won't be back until late next Sunday night—so you can start work again early the next day. Even before you leave, you know it's going to be tough coming back.

Part of you can't wait to leave because you know you're going to have a great time and get away from your normal routine—but the other part would love the chance to piddle around the house, curl up with a great book, start that yoga or exercise program, or maybe take a couple of simple, but relaxing, day trips closer to home. But all that will have to wait because you're going on vacation.

Unfortunately, that other part of you—the part that would love to turn off the phone, play with the kids, clean the closet, avoid crowds, read a book, jog or walk through a local park, plant a garden—rarely, if ever, gets a chance to be nurtured. Your normal life keeps you way too busy, or you're on vacation away from home.

Kris and I had a great home-based vacation several years ago. We agreed that work was off limits—even for one minute during the week. No work-related phone calls would be made or returned—just like we were on vacation. As far as we (and everyone else) were concerned, we *were* on vacation. We turned the ringer on the phone to the "off" position.

We hired a baby-sitter (the kids' favorite person, to make it fun for them) to play with the kids every morning for a few hours while we went jogging together, did yoga, or went out to breakfast. We did several little home projects we had wanted to do for years. We worked in the garden. We sat in the sun and read. It was heavenly. In the afternoons, we did something really fun as a family—hiking, swimming, or hide-and-seek. One day, we hired a massage therapist to give us back-to-back massages, and every night we had different take-out for dinner. We had someone come to the house and help us with the cleaning and laundry—just like being at a hotel. We saw several great movies and we slept in every day. It was like having nine Sundays back to back at a great hotel—at a tiny fraction of the cost!

The kids had a blast, and so did we. We felt as if we finally had the chance to really enjoy our home as a family. The kids were able to see their parent not rushed, at home. (What a concept!) I was more relaxed and rested than I ever remember being after going away for a vacation. And it was so much easier, not only to plan, but to get back into the swing of things once I was back—no travel delays, no lost bags, no jet lag, and no exhaustion from traveling with kids. Because we thought of it as a vacation, we lived like royalty that week—massages, restaurants, a house cleaner, take-out—yet we spent a fraction of what we would have spent flying or even driving to some exotic vacation or fancy hotel. But more than all of that, it was truly special. We realized we work so hard to have a home and to care for it—yet it's so rare that we get to enjoy it without being in a hurry.

I'm not advocating replacing all traditional vacations. I love to go away, and I suspect you do

o. I can tell you, however, that this is a great way to relax, as well as a chance to do things you almost never get to do at or close to home, while spending very little money. As I look at my calendar, I can see that we have another one of these home vacations coming up soon. I can hardly wait.